BEHAVE

The Power of Coach Behaviour in Shaping Athletes' Performance and Personal Growth

Brett White

BE: ACADEMY
where leaders become
www.beleaders.com.eu

Copyright © 2024 Brett White

All Rights Reserved

Paperback ISBN: 978-1-965161-00-5

Dedication

To all the sports coaches who give their time, energy, heart, and soul to developing athletes at every level. Your unwavering dedication, passion, and commitment inspire greatness and foster the growth of both individuals and teams.

This book is for you, in gratitude for your invaluable contributions and tireless efforts to shape the champions of tomorrow.

Thank you for making a difference.

Acknowledgment

This book would not have been possible without the support, inspiration, and guidance of many incredible individuals and organisations.

First and foremost, I want to express my deepest gratitude to my wife, Jenni, your unwavering support, patience, and encouragement have been my rock throughout this journey. To my family, thank you for your constant love and belief in me.

A special thanks to my home football club, Bonnet Bay FC. The camaraderie, passion, and dedication of everyone at the club, from my teammates to the club officials, have been a constant source of inspiration. To the lads in my Premier League team, your spirit and commitment have pushed me to be a better coach and leader.

To HFCA Cambodia, working with you has been an honour and a privilege. The work we do together for the underprivileged and impoverished young people in Cambodia is profoundly impactful, and I am grateful for the opportunity to contribute.

I am deeply thankful to my football friends and inspirations, Paul McStay, Chris Grant, Mick McGovern, Stuart Blake, Sadia Sheikh, Nathan Denham and Paraic Grogan. Your wisdom, experience, and friendship have significantly shaped my approach to coaching and leadership.

A heartfelt thank you to my friend and mentor, John O'Sullivan. Your guidance, insights, and support have been invaluable throughout my career and in the creation of this book.

Finally, to all the sports coaches out there who dedicate their time to developing athletes at every level, particularly those unsung heroes that are coaching kids & youth sports every week, often unnoticed and unthanked—this book is for you.

Thank you all for your contributions and support

About the Author

Brett White is a seasoned sports coach and leadership expert with over 17 years of experience in football (soccer) coaching. He currently serves as the Head Coach for the 2024 Bonnet Bay FC First Grade, leading the team in the SSFA Premier League Men.

Holding an FFA Senior C licence (currently doing his Senior B Licence), he has a rich history of fostering talent and managing large teams, having served as the Coach & Player Development Manager at Bonnet Bay FC from 2014 to 2019, overseeing more than 30 coaches, 600 players, and 42 teams across both men's and women's divisions.

In addition to his extensive coaching background, Brett has dedicated a decade to mindset and resilience coaching at leadership, sporting, and organisational levels. His book, "Sports Mindshift: Building the Character and Mindset of a Champion," published in 2016, has been an encouragement for young athletes seeking to enhance their mental fortitude.

Since 2019, Brett has been the Football Manager at HFCA Cambodia - Happy Football Cambodia Australia, where he works with underprivileged and impoverished young people, using football programs to instil hope and provide opportunities. He is also the CEO and Founder of Be Leaders and the BE Academy, established in 2014, where he continues to develop, train, coach, and empower leaders, teams, and organisations globally.

Brett lives with his family in Sydney, Australia, where he continues to coach and play football, run his business, Be Leaders, and travel frequently to Cambodia to continue his work there with HFCA, and other organisations.

Contents

Dedication.. i

Acknowledgment... ii

About the Author iii

Introduction viii

Section 1 Behave – Coaching Yourself............................. 1

Chapter 1 The Power of Self-Awareness.......................... 2

Chapter 2 The Art of Learning – A Pillar of Exceptional Sports

Coaching.. 5

Section 2 Behave – Coaching Your Players 8

Chapter 3 The Crucial Behaviour of Assertiveness in Sports

Coaching.. 9

Chapter 4 Cultivating Curiosity in Sports Coaching 12

Chapter 5 The Transformative Power of Empathy in Sports

Coaching.. 15

Chapter 6 The Transformative Impact of Effective Feedback in

Sports Coaching... 18

Section 3 Behave – Coaching Your Team....................... 21

Chapter 7 The Core Behaviour of Trust-Building in Sports

Coaching.. 22

Chapter 8 The Essence of Alignment – Crafting a Unified Path in

Sports Coaching.. 25

Section 4 Behave – Coaching Your Leadership 29

Chapter 9 Mastering the Art of Communication – Inclusive, Clear,

and Approachable Coaching. 30

Chapter 10 The Dance of Leadership – Behaviours of Adaptability

.... 33

Chapter 11 The Essence of Decision-Making: Focused,

Conversational, and Considerate Coaching 35

Brett White 38

"Performance is all about behaviour, whether you are an athlete seeking podium or a coach seeking to inspire, motivate and connect with your athletes. Brett White is an experienced coach and mentor who has used sport to change thousands of lives, and his new book is a simple tool kit for establishing transformational coaching behaviours, while minimizing your transactional ones."

- **John O'Sullivan, Founder, Changing the Game Project, USA.**

"Brett has created a resource for an aspect in coaching that is often overlooked and left out of coach education. Managing Self is an important aspect of coaching, maintaining respect, relationships, and standards. Behave is a must-read for coaches who are trying to maximise their impact on their players."

- **Mick McGovern, SSFA Women's First Grade Coach, FFA A Licensed Coach, Head Teacher at Sydney FC Sport & Business Program.**

"Behave stands as an indispensable resource for football coaches at all levels, the knowledge and advice imparted by Brett will not only help the development of their teams but inspire personal growth and leadership excellence."

Paul McStay, Former Celtic Football Club and Scotland International.

"Behave is like having a coach's clinic in your hands. l highly suggest reading with a notepad, because Brett Dispenses titbits of information that can translate to the professional world as well as the world of coaching."

Jon Orr, M.Sc., Founder of the Sports Reclamation Project.

"Behave o.ffers a compelling exploration into the impact of coach behaviour on athlete performance and personal development. With a blend of research, real-life examples, and practical insights, Brett delves into the dynamics between coach behaviour and athlete outcomes, shedding light on the transformative power of positive coaching approaches. This book serves as an invaluable resource for coaches o.ffering actionable strategies for fostering a culture of excellence and empowerment."

Christopher Grant, General Manager at Svay Rieng Football Club (Premier League Cambodia) and Managing Director of Elite Soccer Coaching Cambodia.

"An eye opener for coaches, youth behaviour and leadership."

Sadia Sheikh, Founder DIVA Women FC (first women's football club, Pakistan) and Sports Promoter with Different Places.

"Behave is an outstanding resource for coaches in the sports arena, and l highly recommend it to anyone looking to elevate their coaching skills and make a lasting impact in the realm of sports."

Rukhsar Rashid, Former Pakistan Football Player, Asian Football Confederation "C" License Coach, UEFA Level 1 Football Coach and President at South Youth Soccer Academy.

Introduction

"Great coaches are athlete-centred and person-centred. They recognize that if they connect with the individual and if they coach the person and not the sport, they will reach more of their athletes than by taking a one-size-flts-all approach."

John O'Sullivan. (Every Moment Matters)

In the realm of coach development, I believe there is an area that needs more attention, and that is the exploration and refinement of coach behaviour. It is not simply WHAT we do as coaches that is important; it is also the WAY we do it, and WHO we are when we do.

With over 25 years in the leadership development space, 17 years as a football (soccer) coach, and nine years mindset and resilience coach for leaders and athletes, I've collected insights, observed trends, and absorbed the importance of a coach's behaviour. I have also made plenty of mistakes as a coach along the way, and I am still on that journey. Coaching is more than the execution of tasks; it transcends skills, knowledge, and capacity. It's also about the how, the way we coach, and the essence of our being in those coaching moments.

This book laser-focuses on coach behaviour exclusively, distinct from the development of skills, knowledge, or capacity—although those are undeniably vital aspects of coaching. There's a stack of resources available for honing those areas, but our primary focus is the behavioural foundation of coaching. Whether you're steering a football team, leading a club, or coaching an individual athlete, the significance of coach behaviour cannot be overstated. It is the key to your success, your impact, and the outcomes you aspire to achieve as a coach.

Coaching in sports is leadership. Prominent figures in the leadership domain may not explicitly phrase it as "leader behaviour," but there's a subtle murmur echoing through their insights. The Harvard Business Review recently underscored the urgent need for a shift in leadership development paradigms. Most thought leaders highlight the imperative of focusing on, building, developing, and engaging in the growth of leader behaviour, and as a coach, you are a leader.

Brene Brown, a leading light in the leadership space whom I greatly admire, often delves into the essence of leader behaviour in her podcasts. She emphasizes the pivotal role of behaviour in navigating challenging situations. Ken Blanchard, in his reflections, heralds the undesirability of top-down leadership, advocating for leaders who collaboratively work alongside their teams, fostering growth and achievement.

Yet, despite this chorus, much of the common training and focus remains fixated on a coach's results, often overlooking the crucial aspect of behaviour. This misalignment, I believe, hampers our potential for greater results because it sidelines the crucial interplay between relationships and behaviour.

This isn't an academic exploration; rather, it's a daily practice, an active engagement with tangible strategies, insights, and resources. The cornerstone to unlocking greater potential lies in coach behaviour, particularly in the relationships coaches foster. The influence a coach wields over team engagement is unparalleled. Through this book, I aim to impart practical wisdom, grounded in daily practices. This isn't a random endeavour; it's about consistent, deliberate actions that pave the way for transformation.

Our journey navigates four key spheres of coach behaviour: Behaviour with yourself, with your players, with your team, and with your leadership. These spheres capture the essence of leadership behavioural theories that have evolved over the last century. Within each sphere, we'll explore key behaviours, accompanied by practical daily practices, fostering a holistic approach to coach behaviour development.

Coach behaviour is not exclusive to a select few; it's a universal opportunity. It transcends age, gender, status, title, position, or culture. Everyone, regardless of their background, can embark on the journey of developing these key behaviours. It's an exciting prospect, not just for individuals but for the collective impact that can be realized across clubs, teams, and athletes.

Why invest in coach behaviour development? The benefits cascade across various dimensions-lower turnover of coaching staff and athletes, higher-performing teams and athletes, increased efficiency and productivity, elevated morale, and improved player well-being. These outcomes are not just cost, energy or time-saving measures; they signal a paradigm shift in impact, influence, and results.

As we navigate this transformative journey, I see moments of reflection, challenges, and realisations. Some behaviours may resonate with you naturally, while others may demand introspection and growth. The exciting part is that change is not a distant destination but a daily practice. It's not about occasional actions but consistent, intentional choices.

This is an invitation to a conversation, a dialogue about understanding coach behaviour, its significance, and the practical steps you can take, starting today. I trust that this journey will not just be enlightening but also empowering—a transformative expedition into the realm of your coaching.

Section 1
Behave – Coaching Yourself

Chapter 1
The Power of Self-Awareness

"Be more concerned with your character, than with your reputation."

John Wooden

Welcome to the realm of coaching excellence, where the journey begins with mastering the art of leading oneself – the essence of self-leadership. In this chapter, we'll delve into a pivotal aspect of the behaviour of awareness.

Our focus is on cultivating awareness, a profound understanding of who you are and the changes necessary for personal growth. I firmly believe that change is impossible without awareness. In the exploration of self, we'll unravel two fundamental coach behaviours: awareness and learning. It's fantastic to have you on this journey, so let's explore the intricacies of awareness in a coach's behaviour.

It's crucial to clarify that we're not merely discussing the technical skills a coach possesses; rather, our emphasis is on how those skills are wielded, the way they are executed, and the core identity of the coach. I believe that a coach's profound awareness of themselves and their coaching style is paramount. Self-aware coaches operate with an acute awareness of their behaviours, acknowledging both strengths and blind spots, and understanding the ripple effects of their actions on those around them.

These coaches progressively become attuned to their emotions, fears, and insecurities, recognizing potential roadblocks that may hinder effective coaching. This internal awareness encompasses thoughts, mindset, attitude, and decision-making processes. Self-aware coaches leverage their strengths intentionally and model self-care, fostering an environment of reflection and self-leadership.

The journey to becoming a self-aware coach demands deliberate, daily practices. Learning about oneself, understanding personal wiring, thought processes, and mindsets significantly influence the outcomes a coach achieves. Creating awareness around these elements allows for intentional change.

Being aware of one's behaviour, thoughts, and beliefs can be an arduous and challenging process. Fully aware coaches comprehend their weaknesses and strengths, recognize areas requiring development, and acknowledge behavioural responses in the context of interpersonal dynamics. Are you aware of your beliefs, strengths, and behavioural limitations? What aspects of your behaviour need attention to facilitate the change necessary for personal and professional growth?

Self-aware coaches, in my view, are significantly more effective and impactful. They inspire trust, build alignment, nurture others, and create positive change because they understand the boundaries of their capabilities.

Reflective practices serve as a cornerstone for the development of self-awareness in coaching.

Practice 1 - Be Reflective

The first daily practice I propose is fostering a reflective mindset. Coaches who regularly invest time in reflecting on their journey tend to be more effective. Gratitude journaling is one approach to reflection, helping shift focus to positive aspects even in challenging situations. Asking questions like, "What is my key learning today as a coach?" encourages continuous growth. Reflecting on daily interactions and identifying areas for improvement provides valuable insights.

Practice 2 - Be Brave

The second daily practice involves cultivating bravery. Growing self- awareness requires courage to confront uncomfortable truths. Coaches need to look in the mirror, acknowledge behavioural blind spots, and invite external perspectives. While there may be resistance due to the discomfort of self-discovery, the journey towards awareness demands bravery.

Practice 3 – Be Still

Lastly, the third daily practice is embracing stillness. Amidst the noise of daily life, finding time to be still is essential for reflection and self-awareness. Implementing the practice of diverting daily – taking short breaks for reflection - and withdrawing weekly - allocating longer periods for introspection – creates space for self-awareness. The annual practice of abandonment, where coaches intentionally step away from responsibilities to refresh and restore, complements the daily and weekly routines.

In essence, being reflective, brave, and still daily significantly contributes to the development of self-aware coaching. Remember, it's intentional and consistent actions that bring about transformative change

Chapter 2
The Art of Learning – A Pillar of Exceptional Sports Coaching

"Be a student of the game. Be curious. Always look for opportunities for continued personal development. Listen to, observe and learn from other coaches. Enrol on courses, online resources, webinars, listen to podcasts, etc."

- Tony Elliott

Let's now have a look at another key aspect of sports coaching behaviour-the behaviour of learning. I firmly believe that outstanding coaches are perpetual learners, embodying a commitment to growth through daily expressions of curiosity, contemplation, and attentive listening.

Great coaches live out their commitment to learning daily. This commitment manifests through behaviours such as curiosity, contemplation, and active listening. What distinguishes these coaches is their comfort with uncertainty, the acknowledgment that they don't have all the answers, and an unwavering belief that every moment presents an opportunity to learn.

A defining characteristic of exceptional sports coaches is their possession of a growth mindset. Setbacks and failures are not viewed as insurmountable obstacles but rather as stepping stones for learning and growth. Challenges are seen as opportunities for development, and success achieved by others is a source of inspiration, not a threat.

These coaches approach every situation with a growth-oriented perspective, continuously seeking opportunities for personal and collective advancement. Their resilience stems from viewing setbacks not as defeats but as feedback mechanisms essential for growth.

Being a learner exceeds the act of reading a book; it is a continuous, consistent way of being. It involves a commitment to learning, not confined to specific moments of reflection, or reading.

The heart and art of learning are in the daily behaviours that characterize a coach's approach to life—an approach fuelled by the desire to learn, develop, and grow through every experience, challenge, and interaction.

Understanding that individuals have unique preferences for learning, whether through books, conversations, podcasts, or in-depth study, is crucial. The emphasis lies not on the medium but on the behaviour of learning itself. The key is for coaches to integrate learning practices into their routines intentionally.

Creating a learning culture demands proactive engagement. It requires not only the commitment to lifelong learning but also a deliberate effort to integrate learning practices into daily life. Here are three daily practices that foster a culture of learning:

Practice 1 - Be Observant:

Observation is a skill that can be cultivated instantly. By consciously observing people, stories, processes, challenges, and feedback, coaches develop an inquisitive mindset. Instead of fixating on problems, effective coaches ask themselves, "What can I learn here?" Cultivating a culture of learning involves consistently noticing and interpreting behaviour, outcomes, and contributing factors to success or challenges.

Practice 2 - Be Deliberate:

Change doesn't happen by accident; it requires intentionality. Developing a learning culture is an intentional and deliberate process. Coaches must plan for learning, schedule dedicated time for it, and consistently commit to moments of reflection, reading, or other forms of learning. Information, when coupled with intentional application, leads to transformation. Being deliberate in the pursuit of knowledge ensures continuous growth and development.

Practice 3 - Be Humble:

Humility is the cornerstone of effective learning. Coaches must approach the journey of acquiring knowledge with an open mind, devoid of arrogance or a fixed mindset. Humility ensures that coaches remain open to constructive criticism, feedback, and challenges. It fosters an environment where learning is seen as a collective effort, and knowledge is shared for the betterment of the coach and the athlete, player, team or club.

To build a learning culture within teams and organizations, coaches must be learners themselves. The mindsets and behaviours associated with learning—observation, deliberation, and humility—should be consistently practiced. Reflecting on daily experiences and intentionally seeking opportunities for growth create a culture where learning is not only valued but becomes a source of joy and fulfillment.

As coaches engage in these practices, they contribute to the development of a culture where individuals love what they do, enjoy the company of their teammates, and excel in their endeavours. The journey of becoming a learning coach is an ongoing one, filled with the promise of continuous growth and the realisation of a culture that thrives on curiosity, deliberate action, and humble collaboration. May your coaching journey be marked by these qualities, resulting in outstanding outcomes for you, your players, your team, and your organization.

Section 2
Behave – Coaching Your Players

Chapter 3
The Crucial Behaviour of
Assertiveness in Sports Coaching

"You coach a person, not a sport."

-        **John O'Sullivan**

In this chapter, we'll explore why assertiveness is not only important but a behaviour that should be cultivated, developed, and woven into the fabric of our coaching journeys. Assertive coaches, as we'll uncover, stand up for themselves and others in ways that are not only powerful but also empowering and supportive.

Often misunderstood, assertiveness is more than just being vocal or forceful. It's a delicate balance that requires us to advocate for rights, both ours and those of others, without resorting to aggression, rudeness, or arrogance. This chapter aims to shed light on the significance of assertiveness in coaching, focusing on the way it's expressed.

The essence of assertive coaching lies in its ability to create positive experiences and environments. It goes beyond the mere execution of tasks, emphasizing the importance of how we coach rather than what we coach. A confident and assertive coach does not undermine or belittle but uplifts and invites others into the journey, aligning with the values and culture of the team.

The journey toward assertiveness is, indeed, a developmental one. It involves understanding and appreciating that assertive behaviour, when rooted in self-awareness, is far from ignorant or arrogant. Instead, it serves as a tool to empower and uplift those around us. In the following section, we'll look into the behaviours and daily practices that can help foster assertiveness as a positive force in sports coaching.

Practice 1 - Be Kind

The first daily practice in developing assertiveness is to be kind. Kindness is not merely an occasional act but a daily practice that defines who we are as coaches. The goal is not only to be assertive but also to be known as a kind individual. By filtering our interactions through the lens of kindness, we transform the way we see the world. It's about choosing not to be harsh or judgmental but to empower others, making assertiveness a force for good.

It's essential to recognize that assertiveness and kindness are not mutually exclusive. Even in challenging conversations or crucial discussions, kindness can be the guiding principle, reminding those we coach that our assertiveness is rooted in care and respect.

Practice 2 - Be Strong

The second key daily practice involves being strong. Assertive coaches are strong, moving beyond passive or reactive behaviours to intentional, controlled responses. Strength, in this context, means standing firm against toxic or inappropriate behaviours, making a stand when required, and providing clear direction, particularly in challenging situations.

Being strong does not imply being controlling or defensive. It means being intentional, aware, and responsive rather than reactive. Assertive coaches guide their teams with conviction, especially during turbulent times. The goal is to tell what needs to be said, direct the traffic when chaos ensues, and maintain a sense of control without being domineering.

Practice 3 – Be Respectful

The final daily practice in developing assertiveness is to be respectful. Respect is a two-way street, accommodating different opinions, values, and diverse cultures. Even in moments of assertiveness, it's crucial to maintain respect for people. Disrespectful behaviours lead to disconnection, discouragement, and disempowerment, qualities that hinder effective coaching.

By respecting others, including their cultures, journeys, and stories, coaches create an environment that empowers and invites positive experiences. The daily practice of respect reinforces the understanding that assertiveness when coupled with kindness and strength, fosters a culture of collaboration and mutual growth.

In conclusion, the journey of assertiveness in sports coaching is not about being aggressive or domineering but about being strong, kind, and respectful. These daily practices are not just theoretical concepts; they are actionable steps that coaches can start implementing today. By weaving assertiveness into the fabric of our coaching behaviours, we can become coaches who not only achieve results but also build lasting relationships and positive team cultures.

Chapter 4
Cultivating Curiosity in Sports Coaching

"Coaching is a deeply humanist endeavour, done by humans, with humans, for humans. However, we seem to have stripped the humanity out of coaching in favour of high-performance (whatever that is). Let's re-introduce the soul, depth, and vibrancy of humanity back into coaching."

- Cody Royle

In sports coaching, the journey towards excellence extends beyond technical skills to encompass the behavioural trait of curiosity. Curiosity as a sports coach is a key attribute that distinguishes aware, self-leading coaches.

Curiosity, in my perspective, stands out as a coaching behaviour that is universally applicable and ripe for growth in our roles as sports coaches. I am eager to share insights and daily practices that can be implemented, starting today, to improve the muscle of curiosity within your coaching approach. I firmly believe that intentional and consistent actions foster transformative change, particularly when it comes to developing essential coaching behaviours.

Our focus should extend beyond the technicalities of the game; it should encapsulate how we coach, the way we coach, and the essence of who we are as coaches. Curious coaches exhibit an invitational approach, not only to the external environment but, crucially, to understanding themselves. This intrinsic curiosity forms a cornerstone of the self-leadership journey, intertwining with the first behaviour of self-awareness.

The strength of curiosity in sports coaching reveals itself through active, attentive listening and an eagerness to learn about athletes, experiences, and diverse perspectives. True curiosity ignites a passion for understanding both the external and internal landscapes. It's about asking, "How can I stay curious for just a bit longer?" – a question that can transform decision-making, prevent assumptions, and offer fresh perspectives.

In the coaching journey, curiosity is a choice. Amidst the pressures of tasks, outcomes, and predefined processes, coaches must consciously choose to stay curious. The challenge lies in balancing the desire for results with a sustained commitment to curiosity. A key aspect of this challenge is awareness – understanding your own curiosity level as a coach.

To gauge your curiosity, consider this: How engaged are you with your athletes, coaching staff, and with yourself? The level of engagement should be deliberate, active, and people-driven. Curiosity is intertwined with engagement; the less engaged you are, the less your team will be.

In the pursuit of becoming a more curious sports coach, three daily practices are indispensable:

Practice 1 - Be Engaged

Actively engage with athletes, coaching staff, and yourself. Gauge the level of your engagement – is it active, deliberate, and people-driven? Cultivate a desire to understand and be interested in the stories of those around you.

Practice 2 - Be Inquisitive:

Embrace the power of asking great questions. Develop a repertoire of questions that invite athletes and team members to share more about themselves. Resist the temptation to provide immediate advice; instead, ask one more question and stay inquisitive.

Practice 3 - Be Patient

Practice patience as a daily habit. Be deliberate in listening before speaking, allowing everyone's voice to be heard. Demonstrate patience in team meetings, performance reviews, and all interactions, fostering an environment where diverse perspectives flourish.

As coaches, staying curious means asking more than telling,

Brett White

listening twice as much as speaking, and appreciating the importance of patience. The essence of curiosity lies in the empowerment of others through questions, creating an environment where athletes feel their voices are not only heard but valued.

In conclusion, the daily practices of being engaged, inquisitive, and patient are not just transformative for coaches but also instrumental in shaping a culture of curiosity within sports teams. By developing your curiosity muscle, you embark on a journey of continuous learning, understanding, and empowerment. Dive into these practices, apply them consistently, and watch as curiosity becomes a driving force in your coaching journey.

Chapter 5
The Transformative Power of Empathy in Sports Coaching

"They don't care what you know, until they know that you care.
Personal relationships matter!"

- Luke Meadows

In sports coaching, certain behaviours emerge as essential for creating a positive and impactful environment. These behaviours are not reserved for a select few; they are accessible to all, regardless of where they stand on their coaching journey. Each behaviour, a thread weaving through the fabric of exceptional coaching, holds the promise of transformative change.

In our exploration of crucial coaching behaviours, we turn our attention to empathy—a quality that resonates across diverse cultures and geographical boundaries. This chapter aims to unravel the layers of empathy in coaching, illustrating its profound impact on individuals and teams. Like the other behaviours discussed in this book, empathy is not an elusive trait but a behaviour that can be honed and cultivated by coaches committed to their personal growth.

Empathy in coaching involves connecting with others at a deeper level. It goes beyond mere observation, delving into shared emotions and experiences. This behaviour, demonstrated in outstanding coaches, has universal significance and is evident in various cultural contexts.

Whether coaching in Cambodia, Australia, Pakistan, or Singapore, the resounding message is clear: coaches must embrace empathy. It is the channel through which coaches communicate care, understanding, and engagement with the personal narratives of those they coach. Empathy creates a bridge between the coach and the team, fostering an environment where trust can thrive.

The capacity to listen actively is a pivotal aspect of empathetic coaching. Brené Brown's exploration of empathy versus sympathy provides a valuable perspective. While sympathy involves seeing another's struggles, empathy goes a step further—it feels and connects with those struggles on a profound level. This shift from seeing to feeling is crucial in the coaching journey, as it directs the focus away from problems and processes, placing the emphasis squarely on the person.

Building empathy is not an abstract concept but a journey that unfolds through daily practices. Here are three key practices coaches can adopt to infuse empathy into their coaching every day:

Practice 1 - Be Connected

Brené Brown's assertion that empathy leads to connection underscores the importance of intentional connection in coaching. Coaches must go beyond the roles defined by job descriptions and outcomes and deliberately connect with the person—their stories, challenges, achievements, and perspectives. This requires a daily commitment to prioritizing the person over the process, engaging in genuine curiosity about their journey. Curiosity, as discussed earlier, becomes a catalyst for building empathy, intertwining these critical behaviours in a holistic approach to coaching development.

Practice 2 - Be Listening

Active listening is a cornerstone of empathetic coaching. With one mouth and two ears, coaches are reminded of the importance of listening twice as much as speaking. This daily practice involves understanding the art of active listening, going beyond mere hearing to truly engaging with the speaker's words, emotions, and experiences.

Coaches can cultivate this habit by consciously slowing down, resisting the urge to formulate responses while listening, and committing to understanding before responding. The art of active listening not only deepens connections but also fosters an environment where individuals feel truly heard.

Practice 3 - Be Compassionate

Empathy, when translated into action, takes the form of compassion. Coaches must not only see and feel the person but also act on what they observe and hear. Compassion involves actively engaging in the lives and journeys of those coached. It requires coaches to ask empathy-driven questions, seeking to understand the needs, challenges, and aspirations of individuals. This daily practice invites coaches to be intentional about their actions, creating a supportive and compassionate environment that exceeds the boundaries of sports coaching.

In sports coaching, where relationships between coaches and athletes form the backbone of success, empathy emerges as a non-negotiable coaching imperative. People crave connection, yearning to be seen, heard, and felt. Emerging and seasoned coaches alike, irrespective of their initial thoughts towards empathy, have the power to enhance this critical behaviour.

As coaches, the call to action is clear—develop a greater sense of empathy every day. The journey involves dismantling the barriers of self- perceived limitations and committing to daily practices that prioritise the person over processes, actively listening, and infusing compassion into coaching interactions. Whether naturally empathetic or embarking on a journey of growth, every coach can become better at empathy by embracing these daily practices.

Empathy serves as a vibrant thread, connecting coaches to the hearts and stories of those they coach. As we dive into the practices of being connected, listening attentively, and acting compassionately, we uncover the transformative power of empathy in the journey of coach and player development.

Chapter 6
The Transformative Impact of Effective Feedback in Sports Coaching

"A coach will impact more young people in a year than the average person does in a lifetime."

- **Billy Graham**

In the intricate world of sports coaching, the behaviours exhibited by exceptional coaches can make or break the success of an athlete or team. Among these behaviours, the ability to provide and receive feedback stands out as a key to fostering a positive, growth-oriented environment. This chapter delves into the crucial role feedback plays in coaching, exploring how it can elevate morale, address challenges, and build trust within teams.

Exceptional coaches understand the profound impact of healthy feedback behaviours. They not only celebrate achievements but also engage in effective feedback that addresses areas for improvement. Openness to both giving and receiving feedback characterizes these coaches, creating a culture where continuous improvement is not just encouraged but expected.

Healthy feedback practices are instrumental in preventing performance drift, ensuring athletes stay on course and aligned with team goals. Moreover, feedback serves as a catalyst for conflict resolution, steering conversations toward collaboration, accountability, and stability. This chapter will unravel the benefits that effective feedback brings to the coaching arena.

In sports coaching, the significance of feedback is a recurring theme. In workshops and training sessions around the world, coaches and leaders acknowledge the pivotal role of feedback in team dynamics. It's a conversation that emphasises the universal need for improvement in the way feedback is given and received.

Leadership wisdom underscores the importance of developing positive, effective feedback loops. Exceptional coaches don't shy away from accountability; instead, they embrace it with collaborative approaches that empower, provide permission, and foster stability within their teams. As coaches, we are compelled to examine the feedback culture within our own spheres—whether it be a team, a club, or an organisation.

Acknowledging the profound impact of feedback is only the beginning. Coaches must grapple with the complexities of their own relationship with feedback. The truth is feedback can be a double-edged sword, both loved and feared. While positive feedback is welcomed, the prospect of critical feedback can trigger defensive reactions, challenging even the most seasoned coaches.

In my own journey of coach development, I admit to personal struggles with receiving critical feedback. The reflex to defend oneself, to prove one's worth, is a common human response. However, we need to shift from a defensive stance to an embracing stance of critical feedback. This shift requires a commitment to personal growth and the dismantling of barriers that hinder the acceptance of constructive criticism.

To cultivate a healthy feedback culture, coaches are urged to adopt daily practices that are tangible and applicable. Here are three key practices that can be integrated into the fabric of coaching interactions:

Practice 1 - Be Invitational

Exceptional coaches go beyond merely giving feedback; they invite it. This chapter emphasizes the importance of coaches not only being open to feedback but actively seeking it from those they coach, peers, and even external sources. This invitational approach, when consistently applied, nurtures a culture where feedback is celebrated, valued, and seen as an integral part of growth.

Practice 2 - Be Specific:

Effective feedback is clear, specific, and intentional. Ineffective feedback is vague, generalized and lacks practicality. Coaches are encouraged to provide examples, impacts, and specific instances when offering feedback. This practice ensures that feedback is not a mere exercise in power posturing but a meaningful dialogue that empowers athletes and teams. Always communicate your positive intentions behind the feedback, fostering an environment where feedback is constructive and growth-oriented.

Practice 3 - Be Responsive

The power of feedback lies not just in its delivery but in the hands of the receiver. Coaches are urged to move beyond reactive responses, often driven by emotions, and embrace a reflective and responsive approach. By creating space for reflection, individuals can detach from the emotional charge of feedback, extracting valuable lessons and insights. The goal is to shift from proving oneself to improving oneself—a mindset that aligns with a continuous journey of growth and learning.

The overarching message is clear-effective feedback is a cornerstone of successful sports coaching. It is a behaviour that can be cultivated, refined, and integrated into daily coaching interactions. Coaches are challenged to look beyond the contrast of love and fear in their relationship with feedback and to embrace the potential for growth that it offers.

Our mission of helping coaches become stronger, better, bigger, and brighter resonates in the call to be invitational, specific, and responsive. It's an invitation for coaches to embark on a continuous journey of improvement, not just for themselves but for the teams they coach and the athletes they guide. I'll close with a reminder that building a culture of growth requires intentional daily practices, making feedback a vital tool in the coach's toolkit.

Section 3
Behave – Coaching Your Team

Chapter 7
The Core Behaviour of Trust-Building in Sports Coaching

"Good teams become great ones when the members trust each other enough to surrender the Me for the We."

- Phil Jackson

Throughout this book, our focus has extended beyond the mere execution of tasks; we have looked into the very essence of how coaches conduct themselves and the impact it has on team dynamics. This section navigates through two pivotal behaviours that define exceptional coaches and are intricately connected to cultivating a thriving team culture. Today, we embark on the exploration of the first behaviour - the art of building trust.

Empowering sports coaches recognize that the bedrock of great teams and organizations lies in the cultivation of higher levels of trust. Building trust requires a unique set of skills: a willingness to embrace vulnerability, a commitment to empowering others, and the development of inclusive communication strategies. These coaches establish a culture steeped in honesty and humility, readily admitting mistakes, seeking assistance when needed, and offering sincere apologies when warranted.

The benefits of building trust are substantial - heightened buy-in, constructive conflict resolution, and the formation of cohesive teams that consistently deliver outstanding results. In the coach's playbook, trust emerges as another cornerstone, an indispensable foundation for crafting teams and coach/athlete relationships that thrive in their pursuits.

Research, exemplified by thought leaders like Patrick Lencioni, underscores the pivotal role of trust in team dynamics. The absence of trust, identified as a fundamental dysfunction in Lencioni's renowned work, "The Five Dysfunctions of a Team," hinders the potential for growth and excellence. Without trust, vulnerability becomes elusive, honesty falters, and the ability to navigate conflict, gain commitment, and achieve buy-in is severely compromised.

In the pursuit of high-performing teams that revel in their work, value their teammates, and excel collectively, trust emerges as the foundation. It becomes nearly impossible to construct an environment where passion, camaraderie, and excellence prevail without a sturdy foundation of trust.

Our responsibility extends beyond game strategy and player development; it encompasses the cultivation of behaviours that nurture trust. Trust, however, is a multifaceted concept involving various dimensions — trust in a person's character, capacity, reliability, and sincerity. To be a trusted coach requires vulnerability, a quality that often gets misconstrued as weakness.

Practice 1 - Be Vulnerable

Vulnerability, contrary to popular misconceptions, is a powerful strength in coaching and leadership. Coaches are encouraged to explore the works of Brené Brown, a trailblazer in the realm of vulnerability research. Being vulnerable does not entail the random sharing of personal details; instead, it involves coaching with authenticity, honesty, and accountability. Acknowledging mistakes, taking ownership, and expressing a genuine commitment to growth are all components of embracing vulnerability. By tearing down walls and fostering openness, coaches set the stage for trust to flourish.

Trust is not a quick-fix solution but a long-term investment. Its development is a gradual process that involves crafting a culture deeply rooted in the idea of trust. Furthermore, the fragility of trust demands ongoing efforts to ensure its preservation. Coaches must be attuned to the fact that trust, once shattered, requires genuine honesty, humility, and a commitment to rebuilding.

Practice 2 - Be Sincere

Sincerity emerges as a mark of trustworthiness. In coaching, sincerity is manifested through a consistent alignment of words and actions. Coaches are encouraged to communicate transparently, avoiding hidden agendas and unspoken rules. The depth of sincerity is reflected in the way coaches treat individuals, respect their contributions, and engage in open and honest communication. Sincerity is not merely a behavioural trait; it is a commitment to authenticity in all aspects of coaching.

Practice 3 - Be Caring

To foster trust, coaches must demonstrate a genuine interest in the well-being of their athletes and team members. Prioritising individuals over processes and relationships over results set the stage for a culture where trust can thrive. Coaches are challenged to go beyond transactional interactions, valuing the unique contributions and personal development of each team member. The sense of care and respect becomes a powerful catalyst, inspiring commitment and accountability within the team.

Trust-building is a journey that demands intentional efforts, a commitment to continuous improvement, and an understanding that the way coaches behave is just as vital as what they do.

As sports coaches aspire to foster a culture of excellence, the imperative is clear — trust is critical. The coach's journey involves mastering the art of vulnerability, embracing sincerity, and embodying genuine care. Through these practices, trust becomes more than an abstract concept; it transforms into the lifeblood of high-performing teams and thriving sports organizations. The challenge for every sports coach lies in the daily practice of building and sustaining trust — a commitment that exceeds strategies and plays, capturing the very essence of coaching.

Chapter 8
The Essence of Alignment –
Crafting a Unified Path in Sports
Coaching

"Winning is about having the whole team on the same page."

- Bill Walton

In this chapter, our focus is on the critical behaviour of alignment. The ability to foster alignment within a team or organization is, to me, an essential factor that determines its momentum and forward path.

Exceptional sports coaches understand that building momentum and propelling a team forward is a formidable task in the absence of alignment. These coaches possess the unique ability to organically create alignment within their teams, empowering individuals to function harmoniously. This alignment is forged through shared values, common objectives, and a collective commitment to a cause that extends beyond individual roles.

Creating a scenario where everyone comprehends their part as a vital piece in a larger puzzle, even if the entirety of the picture remains obscured at times, is integral. Aligning the team around a shared purpose, common values, and overarching goals becomes the key to success.

A characteristic of coaches who are good at fostering alignment is their capacity to rebound swiftly from setbacks and failures. While others may falter, coaches who have instilled a sense of alignment witness their teams collectively recovering and persevering. It is not a solitary endeavour; the entire team rallies together, propelled by a shared commitment to the intended goal.

This "all-in" approach is not merely the coach's demeanour; it permeates the entire team. The collective commitment is compelling inspiring and often results in elevated levels of trust. Alignment, in this sense, becomes a source of excitement, a shared journey where every team member contributes to the forward movement.

Alignment is not an abstract concept; it is intricately connected to coaching behaviour and the essence of who coaches are. There are specific behaviours that contribute to heightened levels of alignment. Coaches have the power to engage in actions that build, promote, and lead to alignment or conversely, behave in ways that foster misalignment.

In the vast Australian desert, there's a unique annual event — a canoe race where participants run with canoes in hand, as there isn't any water. This serves as an apt metaphor: when everyone in the canoe runs in the same direction, in harmony and unity, success is attainable. However, if each individual runs in different directions, progress becomes nearly impossible.

Creating alignment is akin to making the journey downstream together. It eases the effort, builds momentum, and fosters a beautiful flow within teams and cultures. Developing daily practices that increase alignment is crucial for team success. It simplifies the journey, accelerates progress, and makes the entire process smoother.

Practice 1 - Be All-In

The commitment to being "all-in" is foundational. Coaches must ask themselves whether those around them will align and buy in if they, as coaches, are not fully committed. Demonstrating commitment, dedication, and an all-in approach every day becomes a coach's responsibility. True coaching is not a part-time endeavour — it requires unwavering dedication and intentional commitment to the team's goal.

Coaches who exhibit a genuine all-in approach inspire confidence and trust. Team members are more likely to align when they witness a coach who is not just coaching from the front but is fully immersed in the journey, committed to overcoming challenges, and dedicated to shared goals.

Practice 2 – Be Purposeful

The concept of purpose, championed by thought leaders like Simon Sinek, plays a pivotal role in fostering alignment. Understanding and embodying the "why" — the purpose behind actions — is essential. Coaches are encouraged to articulate and live out their purpose daily. The power of a purpose-driven coach lies in the ability to inspire and motivate.

Being purposeful involves aligning daily actions with a broader mission. In times of overwhelming challenges, it is the clarity of purpose that provides resilience. Coaches and teams must constantly revisit their "why" to stay focused on the bigger picture. Purpose-driven behaviour, when consistently practiced, fuels motivation, inspires action, and propels teams toward their goals.

Practice 3 - Be Consistent

Consistency is the core upon which great alignment is built. Transformative change does not result from occasional actions; it stems from consistent, intentional efforts. In sports coaching, as in any endeavour, it is what coaches do every day that leads to lasting transformation.

Inconsistency undermines alignment and erodes trust. Coaches must strive to be consistent in their behaviours, practices, and interactions. Team members should not be left guessing about which version of the coach they will encounter each day. A consistent coach builds a sense of reliability, stability, and clarity, which are vital components in fostering alignment.

As we embark on the journey of coaching, the cultivation of alignment emerges as a paramount goal. Committing to daily practices — being all-in, purposeful, and consistent — becomes the pathway to successful alignment. Whether coaching the local under 12's or the Premier League, the principles remain universal.

Alignment is not a destination; it is an ongoing journey that demands intentional efforts every day. As coaches adopt and embody these daily practices, the powerful ripple effect of alignment permeates teams, cultures, and organizations. The challenge for every sports coach is to commit to these practices and witness the transformative impact they can have on creating a cohesive and forward-moving unit. Align, commit, and lead toward shared goals — for it is in alignment that the true power of sports coaching unfolds.

Section 4
Behave – Coaching Your Leadership

Chapter 9
Mastering the Art of Communication – Inclusive, Clear, and Approachable Coaching.

"All the coaches in the world, it doesn't matter how good you are. If your players don't understand what you are looking for or what you want, it makes no sense."

- Pep Guardiola

In our exploration of the critical behaviours of effective sports coaches, we now look into the intricate world of communication—a vital skill that exceeds all coaching capacities. Effective communication is not merely about delivering a message but also about the behaviours that accompany it. In this chapter, we unravel the behaviours that distinguish coaches in their communication, focusing on inclusivity, clarity, and approachability.

While decision-making and communication are both 'what' focused capacities of coaches, the manner in which these tasks are executed plays a pivotal role. A strong coach not only communicates well but also engages in inclusive behaviour, articulating messages that are understood and embraced by the team. Effective communication, therefore, emerges as a cornerstone of successful coaching.

Practice 1 - Be Inclusive

A strength of a great coach lies in their ability to communicate inclusively. Inclusivity goes beyond being a skilled communicator; it's about thinking through the 'who' in addition to the 'how.' Coaches must adopt behaviours that involve people in the communication process. Inclusive communication is not just about delivering information; it's about delivering it to the right people at the right time.

Exclusive communication breeds disempowerment, low morale, and disengagement. Coaches must cultivate the practice of intentionally including individuals in the communication process. Whether through emails, team meetings, or informal interactions, excluding individuals can lead to chaos, disconnect, and a breakdown of trust.

Practice 2 – Be Clear

Clarity in communication is a skill that coaches need to hone daily. Vague generalizations hinder effective communication, and coaches must recognize that individuals process information differently. A great communicator understands the diverse ways people respond and adjusts their communication style accordingly. Clarity extends beyond the spoken word; it involves the tone of voice, body language, and the adaptability to connect with various communication preferences.

Communicatingwithprecisionandawarenessofdiversecommunicati on styles is essential. Whether individuals respond to outcomes, data, or results, a coach must tailor their communication to engage with all types of listeners. The challenge lies in adapting communication to resonate with different preferences, making the workload more demanding but ultimately ensuring that the message is received with depth and clarity.

Practice 3 – Be Approachable

Behaviour is paramount in communication. Coaches must become approachable, fostering an environment where team members feel safe, comfortable, and encouraged to engage. Negative behaviours such as arrogance, ignorance, or aggression hinder approachability. Coaches must consciously choose to respond rather than react, maintaining a calm demeanour and embodying behaviours that build trust and connection.

Approachability is about who coaches are when they communicate. A coach's body language, tone, and overall behaviour significantly impact how their message is received. Reacting emotionally can lead to unhelpful and unresourceful behaviour, while responding thoughtfully fosters an environment of trust, understanding, and alignment.

In the world of sports coaching, communication is not just a means of conveying information; it is the glue that binds teams together, fostering collaboration, trust, and shared success. Coaches who master the practices of inclusivity, clarity, and approachability transform communication from a functional task into an art form that resonates with their teams. As you embark on your journey to enhance your coaching behaviour, remember that the impact of your communication extends beyond the message itself—it lies in the inclusive, clear, and approachable behaviours that accompany it.

Chapter 10
The Dance of Leadership –
Behaviours of Adaptability

"The willingness to experiment with change may be the most essential ingredient to success at anything."

- Pat Summitt

Adaptability is an essential behaviour that sets exceptional coaches apart. Adaptability is not just about adjusting to changing conditions; it's a transformative quality that enables coaches to thrive amidst uncertainty, innovation, and evolving environments.

Adaptive coaches possess a remarkable ability to embrace change. When confronted with shifts in the game, cultural dynamics, team morale, or the overall mood, they exhibit a willingness to adjust. Unlike those resistant to change, adaptable coaches do not get fixated on processes or rules; instead, they remain open to new opportunities.

A prevalent challenge in coaching lies in resistance to change. Many coaches, over the years, have clung to routine and tradition, disempowering their teams. A coach's unwillingness to adapt can stifle creativity, innovation, and the infusion of fresh perspectives within the team. This rigidity, often stemming from insecurity or a toxic approach, erects walls that hinder progress.

The world, much like the sports arena, undergoes continuous evolution. Processes and habits are in a perpetual state of flux. As coaches, if we fail to evolve, we risk becoming stagnant and ineffective. The behaviours that once led to success may not be sufficient in a world that is constantly reshaped by new challenges and opportunities.

The evolution of coaching styles serves as a poignant example. Youth sports coaches cling to outdated methods and risk stagnation. Failure to adapt to innovative coaching techniques, such as incorporating game- like scenarios for skill development, can impede progress. This analogy underscores the broader reality: adaptability is essential at every level of coaching.

Practice 1 - Be Flexible

The daily practice of flexibility requires a coach to recognize the need for change and take actionable steps to create it. Behavioural flexibility demands a departure from repetitive responses to situations. Coaches must challenge themselves to respond differently, fostering personal growth and development. Flexibility is not just a practice; it's a commitment to ongoing adaptability.

Practice 2 - Be Open-Minded

Coaching demands an open mind—open to change, new ideas, and fresh perspectives. While values and beliefs anchor coaches, being overly stubborn or resistant to change can impede progress. Open-mindedness necessitates embracing innovation, risk, and discomfort. Coaches who cultivate this quality invite a culture of continuous learning and evolution within their teams.

Practice 3 - Be Strategic

Strategic leadership in coaching involves navigating between the dance floor and the balcony. (Adaptive Leadership by Ronald Heifetz) Engaging on the dance floor signifies involvement in the daily activities, where the pulse of the team beats. Yet, coaches must also elevate themselves to the balcony, gaining a broader perspective. This dual perspective allows coaches to strategically discern what works, what doesn't, and where innovation is required.

Coaching change is akin to orchestrating a symphony. Adaptability, flexibility, open-mindedness, and strategic thinking are the instruments that, when played harmoniously, lead to a crescendo of success. As coaches in the ever-evolving world of sports, it's our responsibility to cultivate these behaviours daily, ensuring that we stay attuned to the changing rhythm of our teams, organizations, and the world at large. By embracing adaptability, we not only stay relevant but also set the stage for a future where innovation becomes our guiding principle.

Chapter 11
The Essence of Decision-Making: Focused, Conversational, and Considerate Coaching

"Leadership in sport may include a flexible set of skills that engage players. Sometimes, this means being directive, instructional and setting the plays. At other times, it may be sitting back, asking questions, sharing the stage, and allowing the players to create solutions."

- Dan Abrahams

Finally, decision-making is another key behaviour to develop. While skills such as communication are crucial, the key lies in how coaches approach and execute these decisions. In this chapter, we explore the daily practices that distinguish exceptional coaches in decision-making, emphasizing the importance of being focused, conversational, and considerate.

Even accomplished coaches can struggle with adapting their behaviours to enhance the effectiveness of their decision-making. In this last chapter, we focus on the process of decision-making itself— examining not only what decisions coaches make but how they make them and the impact on those around them.

Decisive coaches are good at observation, reflection, analysis, and rapid, effective decision-making. Importantly, they make decisions with people, not for them. The key lies in deep consideration for those in their teams and an understanding of the ramifications of decisions on individuals, team dynamics, culture, and outcomes.

To ensure that decisions are not only made but made in a manner that is healthy, resourceful, and supportive, coaches must adopt key behaviours. The first of these is to be focused.

Practice 1 - Be Focused

Being focused requires intentional effort. Coaches must be attuned to the why behind each decision, understanding and communicating its importance. The behavioural model for decision-making—why, who, what, and how—starts with a deep awareness of why the decision is essential. This clarity becomes the foundation for effective communication and buy-in. Coaches, when faced with impactful decisions, should ask themselves key questions. Why is this decision important? This deliberate process ensures a clear understanding of the decision's significance, creating a foundation for effective communication and gaining support.

Practice 2 - Be Conversational

The art of the coach chat is a critical practice to enhance decision-making. Coaches often make decisions without engaging those who will be affected by them. Exclusive decision-making can lead to feelings of exclusion and disempowerment among team members. Being conversational involves informal, spontaneous chats that bring diverse perspectives into the decision-making process.

Conversational coaches go beyond making decisions in isolation. They actively involve and communicate with those impacted, ensuring their perspectives are considered. These interactions can occur in various settings, fostering an inclusive environment that values the input of all team members.

Practice 3 - Be Considerate

Great coaches acknowledge that every decision, to some extent, creates both opportunities and losses. Deliberate consideration of the impact on individuals is crucial. The "why, who, what, and how" model emphasizes the importance of understanding who will be impacted by the decision.

Coaches must navigate the inherent loss associated with decisions. Acknowledging the change and potential disappointment for those affected is an integral part of being considerate. Engaging individuals before decisions are finalised allows coaches to communicate, empathise, and include them in the decision-making process.

Behave

Decisions are not just choices; they are opportunities to empower, engage, and build a thriving team culture. Coaches who embody the practices of being focused, conversational, and considerate elevate their decision-making from a functional task to an art form that nurtures collaboration, inclusivity, and sustainable success. As you embark on your coaching journey, may your decisions not only lead to victories but also foster a culture where individuals feel valued, heard, and inspired.

Brett White

- 2024 Bonnet Bay FC First Grade, Head Coach, SSFA Premier League Men.

- 17 years of football (soccer) coaching experience.

- FFA Senior C licence

- 2014 to 2019: Coach & Player development manager Bonnet Bay FC, managing over 30 coaches, 600 players, and 42 teams. (Men's and women's)

- Ten years of mindset and resilience coaching in the leadership, sporting, and organisational levels.

- Author of the book, "Sports Mindshift," building the Character and Mindset of a Champion, 2016.

- 2019 to present: Football Manager at HFCA Cambodia - Happy Football Cambodia Australia. Working with underprivileged and impoverished young people through football programs.

- 2014 to present: CEO and Founder of Be Leaders and the BE Academy. Developing, training, coaching and empowering leaders, teams, and organisations around the world.

www.ingramcontent.com/pod-product-compliance
Lightning Source LLC
Chambersburg PA
CBHW061326120626
46546CB00007B/2692